The Dark Side of My Mind

Volume 3

Briana Blair

The Dark Side of My Mind Volume 3

ISBN 978-0-557-76125-8

Contact me: webmaster@bluedragoncreations.com

Visit my website: http://bluedragoncreations.com/gallery/

Table of Contents

Volume 3

Poems 81 - 120

Unwanted - August 1995

I was a girl

Huddled quietly

In my lonely corner

Afraid to speak

Afraid to dream

Small and helpless

I felt unwanted

I am a woman

And now my corner

Is in my mind

I'm afraid to speak

Afraid to dream

Still small and helpless

And feeling

Unwanted

Ugly - *August 1995*

Unsightly

Unseemly

Repulsive

Repellent

Foul and frightful

Misshapen

Misbegotten

Hideous

Homely

Loathsome and horrid

Ugly

I Have No Fear* - *August 1995

I have no fear of dying.

Death is a soft black blanket

That will wrap me in its warmth

When the time comes.

I have no fear

Of the great beyond.

For neither Devils nor Gods

Shall change what I am.

I have no fear of dying.

For death is salvation

From the hell that is Earth,

And I shall embrace it

When it comes.

Pain - August 1995

Words are cracking whips

That scar my tender skin.

Actions are the fists

That bruise my aching flesh.

Oh, glorious pain,

I know you so well!

Throughout my life,

You have been my companion.

And now we meet,

One final time,

As the blade cuts my flesh

And this crimson love flows from me.

And so we move on,

To find new friends.

Oh, sweet pain…

Goodbye.

Speak Not These Words - August 1995

Speak not these words of praise,

For your God is not mine.

Speak nothing of conversion,

For change me you shall not.

Speak n'er of sin and redemption,

For neither matters now.

Say not "you are corrupted",

For I am what I am.

Speak not these words of praise,

For your God is not mine,

But I shall not condemn you,

For each man has his own way.

Paranoia* - *August 1995

The demons roam

In your head

The evil things

The thoughts you dread

You hear them walking

Down your hall

You hear them scratching

At your wall

You lock the doors

Think you're alone

But when you're here

They too are home

Think they're in here

An' coming for ya

But it's just a case

Of paranoia

***Make Love** - August 1995*

Wrap your arms around me

Let your lips touch mine.

Run your fingers down my back

As our bodies now entwine.

Please make love to me.

I want to feel your heart

Beat strongly in your chest,

While you softly kiss my neck

'Cause that's what I like the best.

Please make love to me.

I yearn to feel the heat

Of your body next to mine.

I dream about us sweetheart

Rocking now in time.

So please make love to me.

Where Were You? - September 1995

So long ago,

Yet I remember.

I was in need,

But where were you?

I was hurt,

And I was scared.

I needed help,

So where were you?

I couldn't believe

You weren't there.

I needed you,

But where were you?

And now it's over,

All in the past,

But I still wonder

Where were you?

Sleep: Part 2 - September 1995

I sleep

So deep

In darkness creep

Through dreams

Where screams

Will ring

And bring

The wildest things

To light

At night

And they might

Run free

To see

What there might be

To scare

Out there

As they creep

While I sleep

Cobalt Blue - September 1995

I look your way

And see through you

With my eyes

Of cobalt blue

I see your heart

And it rings true

Beneath a sky

Of cobalt blue

It sprouted wings

And then it flew

Above a sea

Of cobalt blue

And so I see

What is true

With my eyes

Of cobalt blue

Night* - *September 1995

The night

So beautiful

So dark

And inviting

It beckons

It calls

I find it

Delighting

The night

So Sweet

So warm

And right

I feel

So free

I love

The night

To Whom it May Concern **- *September 1995***

To whom it may concern

I'd like to let you know

That we're in an awful mess

Our lives are turning upside-down

For reasons yet unknown

And so I must confess

It's due to all of us

And all the things we do

That things have gone astray

We have to turn this world around

And correct all our mistakes

That's all I have to say.

Little Child - September 1995

All day long

I walked about

Down long roads

Weaving in and out

When then I saw

A little child

And then the child

Began to cry

Her age was

About six years

Her emerald eyes

Were filled with tears

When I looked

And saw her face

She seemed to be

In a far off place

I wish there had been

Something I could do

But not a word I said

To her got through

So I left her

There to cry

But when I left

I knew not why

The Road - October 1995

I see The road before me

Long and winding

And hard to travel

I see the road before me

Long and winding

And begging me to follow

I see the road before me

Long and winding

So far that I cannot see

Where is the end for me?

I see The road before me

Long and winding

And begging me to follow

I see The road before me

Long and winding

Going down 'n 'round

And up and down

The hills and valleys

Of my life

Where is the end?

There is no end

Where is the end?

There is no end

For me

Witch - October 1995

She stands alone

The wind blowing wildly

Through her raven hair

So blue are the eyes

That pierce like darts

With a mesmerizing stare

So sweet is the voice

That whispers your name

And floats on the wind

Enticing is her presence

And the way that she moves

When she walks in

She is a witch

You can't escape her

She has the power

She is a witch

And she'll be 'round

At the midnight hour

The Song Goes On - October 1995

The song goes on

Never ending

Forever sung

By a timeless voice

The words are true

With endless story

Perfectly told

It is your choice

Our song goes on

Never ending

With deepest feeling

Forever sung

A lifelong story

Never ending

Like rock n roll

My Apology - October 1995

Please accept

My apology

I'm not the girl

You thought I'd be.

No longer sweet

No longer clean

I know you know

Just what I mean.

Too much a tease

Too much on fire

I fear no longer

Your heart's desire.

So I submit

Here on my knees

What should I do

To make you pleased?

So please accept

My apology

For not being the girl

You thought I'd be.

Done By Me - October 1995

Why

Is each thing wrong

When done by me?

How

Can things go wrong

And I not see?

Why

Are hearts like stone

When loved by me?

How

Can I ever

Be set free?

Why

Is each thing wrong

When done by me?

How to Change - October 1995

Here is a question

I fear to ask.

Has our sweet love

Come to pass?

Am I demanding

Too much each day?

What shall I do

And how shall I pay?

My sorrow is unknown

For yours is greater, true.

Yet I know no better

What different should I do?

I have hurt our love

For my ways are strange.

But I beg of you

Tell me how to change.

Hold on to Your Dreams - November 1995

Hold on

To your dreams

To your hope

And the fire

That burns inside you

Hold on

To your dreams

Don't let go

Even if

They're hard to follow

So hold on

Just hold on

No matter what

The people say

Your dreams will come

To you someday

When you hold on

To your dreams

And fight

For what you believe

And make your dreams

Come true today

Doors - November 1995

Condemn me

I spoke my mind

Hate me

My views aren't like yours

Degrade me

My life is my own

Exclude me

Just close all the doors

Your prejudice

Is evident

Your destruction

Is imminent

Your hate

Has closed your heart

Your hand

Has closed the door

But someday

You'll see the light

And you

Will hate no more

Scorpion - December 1995

A deadly sting

Comes from this thing

There's only one

The scorpion

Move smooth and quick

That's the trick

To stay alive

Just to survive

His ways are keen

He's rarely seen

And running free

Just like me

No Freedom* - *December 1995

This is the end

My life is over

My dreams

And hopes

And plans

Have all

Come to an end

I have no chance

For anything now

A ball and chain

Have been attached

And all my freedom

Is gone

Forever

Image - December 1995

A young girl and a mirror

A beauty and a beast

Her society says “too ugly”

And her mind agrees

There’s so much loveliness inside her

But this image she so hates

Was harshly cast upon her

By the standards we dictate

And so she asks her mirror

“Why am I so unsightly?

And who will really care

About ‘the beauty deep inside me’?”

And it’s unfortunate to say

So few people ever will

But soon I hope they’ll see that beauty

That lies within her still

The Beast* - *February 1996

In the heart of the beast

Burns the hottest fire

In the heart of the beast

Is a maddening desire.

Evil is his game

And destruction is his plan.

He doesn't have complete control

But he'll do all he can.

He roams around the world

Bringing pain and devastation.

He seems to have such power

How could we find salvation?

This beast is the embodiment

Of our own hate and greed.

And in our present condition

We never will break free.

Nature's Destruction - ***February 1996***

A gorilla mother hides.

She has no tears,

But her heart cries

As she sees her baby die.

They take his head and hands.

A poacher's trophies

That show how modern man

Does not respect this land.

And he doesn't understand

How precious nature is.

And he just won't believe

That this world isn't his.

So another dolphin dies,

And another bamboo falls.

And he will never understand

That it's the death of us all.

Tragedy - February 1996

Everyone is watching

In such great anticipation

As one and all will witness

The miracle of birth.

But I have had to witness

The tragedy of death.

And it's so hard to comprehend

Why so many are so happy

But I must be so sad.

And so I'm left to wonder

Was it something I had done

Or was it simply fate?

All I know for certain

Is that it was a tragedy.

Forbidden Passion* - *February 1996

I am a victim

Of a forbidden passion.

A desperate yearning

For what I can't have.

I dream of carnal pleasures

Beyond those that I know.

I imagine such experiences

As none I've had before.

To have one of my own

If only for one night,

Would it quell my curiosity

Or make me want it more?

So I shall stay a victim

Of my forbidden passion

Until there comes a day

When forbidden it is no more.

The Power of Words - February 1996

These things I write

To some are nothing more

Than mere words on paper.

But words

Are power.

If it weren't for words

There would be no America.

There would be no freedom.

There would be no law.

But many have learned

That the pen

Is mightier that the sword.

And so I shall speak.

And so I shall write.

And so I shall have the power

Of words.

America - February 1996

A man got shot in Dallas.

They found a baby in Bangor.

Drugs are being shipped to Brooklyn.

A woman got raped next door.

There's hunger

And need.

There's crime

And greed.

There's racism

And hate.

There's violence

And rape.

Ain't America beautiful?

Fear - *February 1996*

In the darkness

Beware.

Somebody's

Out there.

You run

And you hide.

But is it safer

Inside?

So you go

Out again.

Is there ever

An end?

It's there

So real.

It's all

You feel

FEAR.

That's the Way - *February 1996*

If you've ever known love

Than you must've known pain

If you've ever seen sun

You must've felt rain

Each thing has a reason

Each thing has a time

The music has its rhythm

The poem has its rhyme

That's the way life is

So for every up

There is a down

But if things go wrong

They'll come around

'Cause that's the way life is

Pain: Part 2 - March 1996

I like the pain

It helps me to know

I'm still alive

For I feel no love

No happiness

Not even sorrow

Ah, but my pain

That, I can feel

For other than my sweet pain

The beautiful lines

I carve along my flesh

There is nothing

A vast emptiness

But my pain fills me

And one day

It will take me to ultimate bliss

In the arms of death.

Sweet Red* - *April 1996

Oh lover,

Let me hold you

And draw you closer

For a kiss.

A sweet,

Deep

Kiss.

Ah, the warmth,

The love,

The blood.

Give me your sweet

Red love

And I

Will give you

Eternity.

I Remember - May 1996

I remember

Your words like daggers

That cut so deep

And left their scars

On my memory

I remember your hate

The needless pain

Inflicted upon my innocence

I remember my agony

As I fought against you

For so many years

But I remember

That I defeated you

And finally

I am free

Life - June 1996

Life

An inextricable maze

A never-ending struggle

Against the rest of the world

Life

A place where most

Exude interminable lies

Without remorse

Life

An extraordinary mystery

That is ending

As soon as it begins

The Dark Road - June 1996

You hope the road is ending

The road of dark and desolation.

But the end for you

Is the start for me.

What will I do

When I'm all alone

Without your touch

Without your kiss

Without your tender voice

To chase away my fear?

What will I do

When there is nothing

But walls

And doors

And emptiness here?

So when the road

For you is bright

Mine will be

In endless night.

Why must life be so cruel?

Can't Lose You - June 1996

Desolation

Desperation

Emptiness

And clinging fear

All alone

And filled with sadness

The time

Is growing near

You'll slip away

Be gone for good

What am I to do?

Please don't leave

'Cause I would die

If I were to lose you.

Money - June 1996

You need it to live

You need it to die

Money

There's never enough

Or never too much

Money

Those who work hard

Will get so little

While those who do nothing

Will get so much

That's why

The greatest corrupter

And the root of all evil

Is money

***Love Forever** - June 1996*

I want you to know

My love is true

My heart beats

For only you

No other could ever

Capture my love

For you are the one

That I'm dreaming of

Never have I

Felt this way

And our love grows stronger

With every day

So Now I say

I'll leave you never

For you are truly

My love forever

www.ingramcontent.com/pod-product-compliance
Ingram Content Group UK Ltd.
Pitfield, Milton Keynes, MK11 3LW, UK
UKHW051134260726
13967UKWH00010B/3039

9 780557 761258